His voice speaks in
soft soul whispers

Charlotte Bonella

This book is a work of non-fiction. Unless otherwise noted, the author and the publisher make no explicit guarantees as to the accuracy of the information contained in this book and in some cases, names of people and places have been altered to protect their privacy.

WestBow Press books may be ordered through booksellers or by contacting:

WestBow Press
A Division of Thomas Nelson & Zondervan
1663 Liberty Drive
Bloomington, IN 47403
www.westbowpress.com
844-714-3454

Because of the dynamic nature of the Internet, any web addresses or links contained in this book may have changed since publication and may no longer be valid. The views expressed in this work are solely those of the author and do not necessarily reflect the views of the publisher, and the publisher hereby disclaims any responsibility for them.

Any people depicted in stock imagery provided by Getty Images are models, and such images are being used for illustrative purposes only.
Certain stock imagery © Getty Images.

Scriptures are taken from The Living Bible copyright © 1971 by Tyndale House Foundation. Used by permission of Tyndale House Publishers Inc., Carol Stream, Illinois 60188. All rights reserved. The Living Bible, TLB, and the The Living Bible logo are registered trademarks of Tyndale House Publishers.

ISBN: 979-8-3850-4166-4 (sc)
ISBN: 979-8-3850-4167-1 (hc)
ISBN: 979-8-3850-4168-8 (e)

Library of Congress Control Number: 2025900119

Print information available on the last page.

WestBow Press rev. date: 01/29/2025

WESTBOW
PRESS®
A DIVISION OF THOMAS NELSON
& ZONDERVAN

Acknowledgments

———◆◆◆———

Where do I begin?

Thanks to all who encouraged me. Your positive words sustained me. Thanks to those who discouraged your words were often remembered and pushed me onward. Christine, pastor Marco, Carrie, Lana you were so pivotal in seeing this through. Very special thanks to Sidney!! Your understanding, patience, incredible artistic insight, amazing computer skills and did I mention PATIENCE!! Saw this over the finish line. Heartfelt thanks to you all!

But they that wait upon the Lord shall renew their strength. They shall mount up with wings like eagles; they shall run and not be weary; they shall walk and not faint. ~Isaiah 40:31(TLB)

Dedication

———◆———

My heart has heard you say "Come and talk with me, O my people" and my heart responds "lord, I am coming."
~ Paslm 27:8 (TLB)

Soft soul whispers! What did you say??? Are we so consumed by life; worried, depressed? Have we become numb? Are we "hard of hearing", grown deaf to the quiet Spirit that whispers?

My prayer, that words written here might cause you to ponder, to quiet yourself, and listen for that soul whisper that guides, inspires, activates and renews!

Think about yourself! How are you with God the Father, Jesus the Son and the comforter of our souls, the Holy Spirit?

Consider forgiveness never ending! Love all enduring, peace in all things and life eternal!

Reach out! Call out! Jesus is near, nearer than you think.

Sometimes our souls perceive, what our minds can't handle.

So get rid of all that is wrong in your life, both inside and outside, and humbly be glad for the wonderful message we have received, for it is able to save our souls as it takes hold of our hearts. ~ James 1:21 (TLB)

All things

———◆►◄◆———

*What a god is he! How perfect in every way. All
his promises prove true, he is a shield for everyone
who hides behind him. ~Paslm 18:30 (TLB)*

The lord is all things
Consuming fire
Mercy on dove's wings

Love we cannot measure
Holiness and grace
All knowing, healing, savior
You took our place

Shepherd, King
Counselor, Father
Forgiving and mighty
In our darkest hour!

In your presence
Forever humble
Your guarding spirit
Softens our stumbles

Love, Salvation
Gentleness and Strength
Holy fabric of
Our faltering faith

Thank you for
Our daily portion
Forever grateful
We offer devotion

Power and glory
Yours forever will be
Majestic god
Holy Father of me.

Holy Father Of Me

Fear not, for I am with you. Do not be dismayed. I am your God. I will strengthen you; I will help you; I will uphold you with my victorious right hand ~Isaiah 41:10 (TLB)

Don't you yet understand? Don't you know by now that the everlasting God, the Creator of the farthest parts of the earth, never grows faint or weary? No one can fathom the depths of his understanding. ~Isaiah 40:28 (TLB)

Mover of mountains
Master of seas
King of Heaven
Holy Father of me

You tap on my hearts door
Softly you come
Announcing your presence
Holy three in one

You bring gifts of mercy
Forgiveness and love
My helper, My refuge
Sweet peace from above

My heart opens wide
I ask you to stay
Gladly your servant
Humbly I pray

This day forever
And ever you will be
My master, My savior
You set me free

Mover of mountains
Master of seas
King of Heaven
Holy Father of me!

Mystery

If you love me, obey me; and I will ask the Father and he will give you another Comforter, and he will never leave you ~John 14:16-17 (TLB)

Within this broken,
Earthbound ware,
A high and holy treasure.

Oh, mystery of mysteries.
And grace beyond
All measure.

The Lord is in
His holy house,
Mysterious habitation.

I feel His presence,
Here within,
I offer adoration.

Keep burning essence,
Of my soul.
Keep cleansing me oh lover.

I want to serve.
To praise my God.
Forever and forever!

God's Essence

What is this stirring, deep within?
That seeks to comfort and hates my sin.
Glorious God, you stooped so low,
A drop of essence placed in my soul.

You put it there to be my guide.
Faithful companion, to steer and guide.
It brings great joy just to know,
Jesus, your son, loves us so.

You did not abandon me to death.
To struggle here to find the path.
The Holy Spirit, one of three,
A comforter for wretched me.

Dwells within. and if I but ask
Will be a part of every task.
Not by power, not by might.
But by your Spirit, I fight the fight.

Your love and mercy unending flows.
Your grace extended to me below.
May I forever grateful be,
Your Spirit essence dwells in me!

The Vessel

———◆◆◆———

And yet, O Lord you are our Father. We are the clay and
you are the potter. We are all formed by your hand.
~ Isaiah 64:8 (TLB)

The potter came to work today,
And toiled over his mounds of clay.
Just water and mud,
A voidless mass.
He sat at his wheel,
Worked at his task.

He makes many vessels,
For all uses.
They line his shelves.
He mass produces.

Some for beauty,
Some just pots,
Many discarded,
With too many flaws.

But then…

The Master potter came.
He knew each voidless mass by name.
He lovingly formed them,
With His hands.
And for each one,
He has a plan.

He wants to fill them
With His glory.
To overflow
And tell His story.
Sins forgiven by Christ God's son,
Our vessel life has now begun.

There will be chips, cracks and falls,
The Master potter
Will mend them all.
He heals, restores,
Sets us aright,
To carry on our holy fight!

And when He turns this vessel over,
Its use on earth forever done.
Stamped on its base,
In holy blood,
Redeemed by love,
Father, Spirit, and Son!

11

The Seed and the Son

But grow in spiritual strength and become better acquainted with our Lord and Savior Jesus Christ.
To him be all glory and splendid honor, both now and forevermore. ~2 Peter 3:18 (TLB)

I am no different
Than a little seed
Seeking the warmth
Of the Son on me.

I am no different
Than a little sprout
I wasn't sure
How I'd turn out

Seeking the son
On my upward path
Up I grew
A struggling shaft

The buds came
Flowers bloomed
I can't believe
How that seed grew!

And though leaves fade
And petals fall
God's son remains
Holy Father of all!

I am no different
Than a little seed
Seeking the warmth
Of the Son on me.

Heart Song

————◆————

Create in me a new, clean heart, O God,
filled with clean thoughts and right
desires. ~ Psalm 51:10 (TLB)

My fickle heart,
Yes, it is so,
So easily tossed,
To and fro.

Yes, man's intentions,
Though good they be,
Oft are not centered,
Wholly on Thee.

We strive, we fuss,
We carry on.
We've lost the focus,
Of our heart song.

Yet in loving kindness,
You redeem.
Yesterday, today,
Forever the same.

I seek your spirit,
To take control.
Filled with your peace,
My only goal.

Lord take it all.
Help me stand.
On solid rock,
Held in your hand.

Until my last breath,
When're it be.
Forever my heart song,
To be with Thee.

Home

Do not fear for I am with you, do not be dismayed for I am your God. I will strengthen you; I will help you; I will uphold you with my victorious right hand.
~Isaiah 41:10 (TLB)

A word that inspires.
Memories, sadness, joy, adventures, triumphs, and losses are all a part of "home".

In this time of masks, distancing, loneliness and isolation we long for
gentle touches and strong hugs from those who love us; for laughter and
it's sweet embrace. Closeness is missing. We all suffer from it's loss!

Celebrations put on hold. Our mourning put on hold. Babies
born. Birthdays missed. Old ones isolated, dying.

Dear Lord. We dream of life restored. We remember home!

Hope

*What's more, I am with you, and will protect you
wherever you go, and will bring you back safely
to this land; I will be with you constantly until I
have finished giving you all I am promising.*
~Genesis 28:15 (TLB)

War, Tragedy
Strikes again
Taking lives
Crippling men

In the dark
The children cry
Lover's weep
Old ones sigh

Homes are gone
Cupboards bare
A weeping soldier
kneels in prayer

Yet in the black
A tiny spark
Made brighter still
In all this dark

A golden beam
From God's own hand
That bids us come
And helps us stand

What is this
This spark
This light

It is HOPE!

Fear

———◆◆◆———

Don't be afraid, for the Lord will go before you and will be with you; he will not fail nor forsake you.
~ Deuteronomy 31:8 (TLB)

I am holding you by your right hand—I, the Lord your God—and I say to you,
Don't be afraid; I am here to help you. ~Isaiah 41:13 (TLB)

There is no fear
Can conquer me
A child of God,
He lives in me.

I feel His presence,
Deep within,
I am safe,
Cleansed from sin.

He owns the sunrise,
And all it brings,
Through good and bad,
To Him I cling.

And at the sunset,
The day now spent.
I rest in Him.
And am content.

May I ever humble be.
Thankful that
You live in me.

There is no fear,
Can conquer me,
A child of God
I've been set free.

Peace

Don't worry about anything; instead, pray about everything; tell God your needs, and don't forget to thank him for his answers. If you do this, you will experience God's peace, which is far more wonderful than the human mind can understand. His peace will keep your thoughts and your hearts quiet and at rest as you trust in Christ Jesus.
~Philippians 4:6-7 (TLB)

I am distressed
Downcast, torn,
From life's battles
Weary and worn.

My leaking soul.
Is aching, shriveling.
I need you Lord
To go on living.

You still hear,
My weakened pleas.
Your forgiveness and mercy,
Renew me.

You bid me come,
My soul hears.
Your gentle arms,
Calm my fears.

I hear Your voice,
"Fix your eyes on Me.
I love you child.
Be still. Follow Me!"

The Race

Since we have such a huge crowd of men of faith watching us from the grandstands, let us strip off anything
that slows us down or holds us back, and especially those sins that wrap themselves so tightly around our
feet and trip us up; and let us run with patience the particular race that God has set before us.
~ Hebrews 12:1 (TLB)

Strip off all
That impedes your pace.
For you are in
A heavenly race.

Things that want
To make us fall.
Lose our focus,
Lose it all!

Jesus on the cross
You groaned.
Now you sit
Upon the throne.

God the Father,
You bid us come.
To stay the course,
With patience run.

That we will one day
Be with Thee
At peace in glory,
Heavenly!

It will be home,
Our final place.
We'll look upon,
Your mercy face.

So come believers.
We are free.
We have a goal.
Sweet destiny!!

Don't be tangled,
Tripped or stray.
Stay the course.
So that we may

Run with patience
The course is set
Hold His promises
And not forget!

I will be with you.
Will always be.
To the end of the earth,
And all eternity!

The Plan

***

He will keep in perfect peace all those who trust in him, whose thoughts turn often to the Lord!
~Isaiah 26:3 (TLB)

But for good men the path is not uphill and rough! God does not give them a rough and treacherous path, but smooths the road before them. 8 O Lord, we love to do your will! Our hearts' desire is to glorify your name. 9 All night long I search for you; earnestly I seek for God; for only when you come in judgment on the earth to punish it will people turn away from wickedness and do what is right.
~Isaiah 26:7 (TLB)

It's lonely here
Swaying to and fro
At the top of the ladder
Now where do I go?

I've fulfilled my goals
Climbed to the top
It's lonely here
I've come full stop

This ladder is shaking
I'm going to fall
Then a saving hand
Stills it all!

You've forgotten Me
Says a gentle voice
Not considered Me
In any choice

Is this where
You want to be
A life devoid
And far from Me

I offer forgiveness
And by my grace
We can rebuild
At my spirit's pace

There will be trials
But peace prevails
It will soothe, inspire
So set your sails

No greater goal
Could ever be
To spend each moment
Each breath
With Me

Though sovereign king
I AM of all
And you a speck
A creature small.

I love you lost one
Who cannot see?
You're My treasure
So lovingly

I hold you in
My mighty hand
And for your life
I have the PLAN!

Life is the Pits

God is our refuge and strength, a tested help in times of trouble.
~Psalm 46:1 (TLB)

Because he bends down and listens, I will pray as long as I breathe!
Death stared me in the face—I was frightened and sad.
~Psalm 116:2-4 (TLB)

He has saved me from death, my eyes from tears, my feet from stumbling.
~Psalm 116:8 (TLB)

We have all heard this expression, used it. To me pits are things like despair, anger, jealousy, hatred, self-ridicule, addiction, greed and pride to name a few. The list goes on, on and on!

Pits only go one direction: down, down, down. They have slippery, slimy edges. It's difficult to get a grip. They are dark and getting darker.

One can continue to spiral. But I say look up. There is light up at the top. Cry out to God! He has promised to bend down and listen!

He is the author of love, patience, strength, forgiveness. He actually inspired a book on these very subjects! The HOLY BIBLE.

Slowly one step at a time, then another and one more. One good grip then another, He will guide you back, and lift you up! He will cradle you in His arms and set your feet on solid rock!

DANGER: AVOID PIT STOPS!

Caught and Released

———◆———

I waited patiently for God to help me; then he listened and heard my cry. He lifted me out of the pit of despair, out from the bog and the mire, and set my feet on a hard, firm path, and steadied me as I walked along. He has given me a new song to sing, of praises to our God. Now many will hear of the glorious things he did for me, and stand in awe before the Lord, and put their trust in him.
~ Psalm 40:1-4 (TLB)

I am caught in the muck,
Of my despair.
There is no light,
There is no one; there.

Deeper and deeper,
It sucks me down.
The walls so slippery,
Darkness; profound.

In a last moment,
I seek God's face.
Pull me out Lord,
Then by His grace.

Slowly, steadily,
We upward climb.
Free of the pit,
Its mire and slime.

The Lord is merciful,
Strong and kind.
Puts my feet on rock.
Heals my mind.

There is a new song,
It fills my soul.
A hymn of praise,
I am made whole!

Webs

———◆━◆━◆———

Don't copy the behavior and customs of this world, but be a new and different person with a fresh newness in all you do and think. Then you will learn from your own experience how his ways will really satisfy you.
~ Romans12:2 (TLB)

My mind scurries to and fro
Fraught with care
Intentions, woe

White noise is everywhere
Your voice Lord
Is hard to hear

I`m entangled
In worries webs
Filled with fear
Sadness, dread

But I choose to stop
And quiet be
Let your voice
Speak to me

In the quiet
What do I hear?
Songs of birds
Gentle breezes stir

Your love comes
In soft soul whispers
Calms my mind
Soothes life`s blisters

Be not deafened
By this worlds noise
Seek me instead
Hear my voice

I love you child
Give your cares to me
I am the One
I`ll set you free!

How Can It Be

To all who mourn in Israel he will give: beauty for ashes; joy instead of mourning; praise instead of heaviness. For God has planted them like strong and graceful oaks for his own glory. ~Isaiah 61:3 (TLB)

I walk on earthly dust bound roads
And Jesus walks with me
Joy from sorrow
Beauty from ashes
Oh, divine alchemy!

He is always present
Though I cannot see
His spirit whispers
I'm here with thee.

My name is written
On His hand
What peace
Floods my soul

Broken pieces mended
Hope restored
Forgiven ....safe
Whole!

The Gift

So get rid of all that is wrong in your life, both inside and outside, and humbly be glad for the
wonderful message we have received, for it is able to save our souls as it takes hold of our hearts.
~ James 1:21 (TLB)

What is this warmth
That softly glows
Invades my secret
Inner soul

Peace and love
That calms my fears
Gives blessed hope
And brings my tears

Forgiveness, holy gift
In all its glory
Freely given
Rewrote the story

Of my life
Once scarred and sad
I now rejoice
And am so glad

For it has saved
My very soul
Cleansed, redeemed
My heart made whole.

Holes

———◆✕◆———

So let us come boldly to the very throne of God and stay there to receive his mercy and to find grace to help us in our times of need.
~Hebrew 4:16 (TLB)

I love the Lord because he hears my prayers and answers them. Because he bends down and listens, I will pray as long as I breathe!
~Psalm 116:1-2 (TLB)

See my life,
So full of holes.
Failures and needs
Have taken a toll.

I strive for success.
Seek lofty goals.
And yet I fall short.
I'm so full of holes.

I dress up my outside.
Put a smile on my face.
My inner soul cringes.
At all my mistakes.

My great gaping holes.
You seek to fill
My neediness draws you,
Your love to instill.

My yielded heart
Will not whine or rebel.
I choose to thank you.
When all is not well.

You claimed me from death.
My eyes from their tears.
My feet, saved from stumbling.
Whom shall, I fear!

Thank you, dear Jesus.
you forgave and made whole.
You've filled up my life.
Once so full of holes.

Faith

———✦———

We know these things are true by believing, not by seeing
~2 Corinthians 5:7 (TLB)

What is faith? It is the confident assurance that
something we want is going to happen. It is the
certainty that what we hope for is waiting for us
even though we cannot see it up ahead. Men of
God in days of old were famous for their faith.
~Hebrews 11:1-2 (TLB)

Where is the faith
That was so bold
So famous in
God's men of old

To look ahead
Though we cannot see
Ours hopes
And dreams
Are known to thee

In the present
We are perplexed
Grasping, praying
About what's next

Your love holds us
You've planned ahead
We will go bravely
Where we fear to tread

Lord you are
Our steadfast hope
Though unseen
Your love we know

You lead and guide
You encourage us
We have your words
Your spirit in us

We will walk
In the light you give
Focus on you
To help us live

Faith it grows
From day to day
What lies ahead
We cannot say

God your heaven
Is what we seek
We give our souls
To you to keep

There is much faith
It makes us bold
We are no different
Than God's men of old

Nature

See the lily,
Pure and white.
Escape its bud
To share its light.

I am in
The baby's cry
Deep dark valleys
Blushing skies

Behold my glory.
In all things.
Flowers that bloom.
Birds that sing.

I am here!!
I created wonder!

God's Classroom

Look the dawn has come!
It's first gold spears,
Heralding the day.

Forests scented,
With pine and fern.
Wilderness covered,
In moss blankets.

Fists of mountains,
Seeking the heavens.
High and mighty,
Great rocks they are.

The waves roll,
On and on.
The vastness of the ocean,
Proclaimed!

Brush strokes,
Streak across the sky.
Painting crimson and yellow,
Sunset's canvas never repeated.

Thorn's pierce.
Yet we seek the rose's beauty.
Petals soft, alluring,
Fragrance profoundly gentle.

Creation …
God's pallet,
It's rough mud
His to shape.

Stop! Sense! See! Listen!
Creation beckons,
If we but awaken
To the masterpiece!

My Garden Prayer

Be beautiful inside, in your heart, with the everlasting charm of a gentle and quiet spirit which is so precious to God.
~1 Peter 3:4 (TLB)

Dear Lord: Like the morning glory opens to you each morning, I will raise my head in honour of your holy presence. The sunflower follows the sun seeking light and warmth. So may I seek your blessing, warm and bright, all the day long.

May I have the heart and persistence of the dandelion, never giving up, bringing a spot of colour wherever I go. Happily blooming in the ugly places, the country clubs and the alleyways.

The thistle is prickly and the nettle stings. Forgive my harsh words and thoughtless deeds. May my presence soothe and calm like lavender, chamomile and peppermint. May the sweet fragrance of your spirit surround all I do, like peony, lilac and honeysuckle.

May I not be detested like weeds but treasured like the first bud on the rosebush. The winding ivy covers the bare places in my garden. I pray for a quiet, listening spirit that can fill the gaps and stretch beauty across the dark barren places in those around me. Give me your grace.

May I be more like the lily, not worrying about tomorrow. I will be content in how you created me, not always looking to be different.

Lord I ask that my roots grow deep in your love and that my stems be strong to resist life's storms. May my blooms glorify this garden's Holy Keeper.

White fragrant blossoms foretell the coming of fruit, peach, pear, and apple. I thank you for the tiny seeds planted and what they will bear.

Winter will come, and for a season this garden of my soul will be silent. I look forward to awakening, warming in the light of God's son and taking my place in His eternal garden.

We praise you and thank you for new life, renewed hope, and eternal peace. Amen

The fountain

For you are the fountain of life
our light is from your light.
~ Paslm 36:9 (TLB)

There is a fountain
in my garden
its trickling waters
soothe my soul
beast and bird
stop and ponder
drink their fill
then on they go.

There is a fountain
in gods garden
filled with blessings
to refresh and cleanse
its never-ending grace
flows freely
trickling mercies
pardon me.

When I'm parched
to the fountain I come
waters refresh, restore
peace drenches me
forever grateful
forever humble
his grace fountain
flows free for me.

Yes, there is a fountain
in gods garden
its trickling waters
soothe my soul
and by his love
I am pardoned
I'll stop, drink deep,
Inspired I'll go

I Sing

In the shadow of your wings, I sing for joy. I cling to
you and your hand keeps me safe.
~ Psalm 63:7-8 (TLB)

I sing in the shadow of your wings
To you I cling
You hold me with your right hand
You are my help.

I sing because you are with me
I only need focus on you
Clear my mind
I give you, my heart.

I sing because your light shines on my path
As it twists and turns
Uphill and down
You are always there.

I sing because you are my hope
Today and everyday
You never change
You`re promises stand.

I sing because you are life
Now and eternal
Promises enduring
Forever the same.

I sing because I am thankful,
In joy and praise I worship,
You fill me to the full
Thank you Lord.

God Behind the Glass

In the same way, we can see and understand only a little about God now, as if we were peering at his reflection in a poor mirror; but someday we are going to see him in his completeness, face-to-face. Now all that I know is hazy and blurred, but then I will see everything clearly, just as clearly as God sees into my heart right now. ~ First Corinthians 13:12 (TLB)

The glass is blurred.
I cannot see.
The image there,
In front of me.

I sense its power.
I feel its glory.
Peace, mercy, love,
A wondrous story.

I love you Lord.
I'll trust, obey.
Your will for me,
I'll seek each day.

One day soon,
The glass replaced.
I'll see you clearly,
Face to face.

The Lost Ones

Be delighted with the Lord. Then he will give you all your heart's desires. ~Psalm 37:4 (TLB)

Like sheep you wandered away from God, but now you have returned to your Shepherd, the Guardian of your souls who keeps you safe from all attacks. ~ 1 Peter 2:25 (TLB)

My heart aches,
Everyday.
For dear ones,
Who've gone astray.

Wandering, sighing,
Sad and lost.
Seeking pleasure,
At any cost.

Their faces show,
Their inner pain.
A spirit aching,
To be whole, again.

God has promised,
In his words.
He'll seek the lost.
Their hearts he'll stir.

I will find those sheep
So, all alone.
Love and guide them.
Bring them home.

Pray without ceasing,
Everyday.
I will restore them.
They'll find their way.

I will mend
Their broken souls.
Love and restore,
Make them whole.

I am God!
Give them to me.
I am the shepherd,
Who'll set them free!

Me and My Shadow

————◆✦◆————

He has promised
He's always there
Nothing can separate
His words are clear.

So let me take
Another step
Earthly shackles
Start to slip.

In His care
There'll be a way
I trust you Jesus
Lead the way.

Yes
I see it now
Light on the way
To show me how.

Put my worries
Down a while
Focus my mind
On His love and power.

Separate?
Not death, life, angels, hell
Ever constant
His love prevails!

Forever grateful
Yes I'll be
Forever present
He shadows me.

Prayer

In all you do put God first…he will direct you and crown your efforts with success.
~Proverbs 3:6 (TLB)

Open my eyes,
Help me see.
Clearly the path,
You have for me.

Open my ears,
Let me hear.
Nature's sweet music,
Pure and clear.

Open my heart,
Fill it with love.
Mercy and grace,
That comes from above.

Open my mind,
Refresh and renew.
May all I do,
Reflect only you!

Amen

Not One Sparrow

Not one sparrow (What do they cost? Two for a penny!)
can fall to the ground without your Father knowing it!
~ Matthew 10:29 (TLB)

Take heart!
The Father is near.
Sees our distress.
Understands our fear.

He offers peace.
If we but seek.
Quiet release
For the tired, sad, weak.

Yes, be assured.
He's in it all
Sees the sparrows
When they fall

Not one is lost.
From His gaze
His hands are open.
To bestow His grace.

So, rest in Him.
His mercy endures
Love never ending
Eternal, secure.

Not one sparrow.
The least of all
He knows, forgives
Softens our fall.

Take heart!
The Father is near.
Sees our distress.
Understands our fear

Christmas Eve

—◆◆◆◆◆—

Two words – "Christmas Eve" and memories begin to surface!

As a child I never realized we were poor. Yet our parents made this night special. Of course there was a church Christmas pageant, baking, company, singing, laughter and a present for each of us.

In my own home Christmas Eve was chaos! There were two shepherds and one angel to make ready. The angel lost a shoe, there was paper and ribbons and bows everywhere. The dog ate the butter tarts and the local Santa was knocking at the door! My Mother-in-law was coming.

But not all Christmas Eves were exciting. I can't help but remember the loneliness, overwhelming sadness, heartache so intensified on this night!

Some can't wait for Christmas to come – others can't wait for it to end!

2000 years from now, our birthdays will be forgotten. Christ's birthday ordered the years of men. BC, AD – the whole world agrees on what year it is!

We celebrate His arrival on earth, every year; ticking off the decades and centuries. We remember His humbleness and divinity, all rolled into one! Yes Christmas Eve has come again!

Christmas Eve has Come Again

Christmas Eve has come again
Fussing, frenzy,
Complete mayhem.

Little angel has lost her shoe
There's a mess on the floor
The dog is sick
Santa is at the door!

Company is coming!
….No one is coming….
Lights, laughter, presents!
…A wounded heart weeping…

Christmas Eve has come again
The birth of Christ
Orders the years of men.

Angels, shepherds
A star in the sky
Mary, Joseph
Tiny savior's soft cry.

Christmas Eve has come again
Sacred sacrifice
Come down from Heaven
Hope was born
This night!

He lived love and peace
Taught us to forgive
His words still teach us
How to live!

So lets bow our heads
And bend a knee
And worship the birth of DEITY!

Silent Night!
Holy Night!

Christmas Eve has come again!

Christmas Bells

———◆———

Listen! The virgin Mary shall conceive a child!
She shall give birth to a Son and he shall be called
"Emanuel (meaning God is with us)."
~Matthew 1:23 (TLB)

Listen, listen!
Can you hear the bells?
Listen, listen!
To the story they tell.

Of shepherds awake,
On a cold silent night.
Watching their sheep,
In the midnight starlight.

The heavens burst forth,
With light, angels and sound!
They were so afraid.
They fell to the ground.

"Arise!
Gentle shepherds."
"Arise!
Have no fear."

"The Messiah,
The King babe,
He is born
He is here!"

"Follow this star
To the place where he lay."
'In a Bethlehem stable
Asleep in the hay!"

Listen! Listen!
Can you hear the bells?
Listen! Listen!
To the story they tell.

Of a beautiful mother,
Holding her baby close.
Kissing his sweet head.
And counting his toes.

Her heart filled with wonder.
Her heart all astir.
She looks down in love.
And God looks back at her!

Joseph knelt down,
In the lowly cow stall.
Cattle, sheep, Mary,
Baby and all.

He touched tiny hands.
He named Him Jesus.
Savior, Immanuel,
God is with us!

Jehovah, Messiah,
Great God of all.
You sent your love,
In a package so small.

Listen! Listen!
Can you hear the bells?
Listen! Listen!
To the story they tell

Of wise men who came
From faraway lands
Following a star
With gifts in their hands

They sought the child
That the prophets foretold
Knelt, worshiped, gave gifts
Myrrh, frankincense and gold

They cautioned His parents
Of an evil king's plan
Then slipped away quietly
And returned to their lands.

Listen! Listen!
Hear the bells ring!
Listen! Listen!
To the message they bring

Of the boy who grew,
And became a man.
He calmed the sea,
With a wave of His hand

He turned water to wine,
Made blind men see.
Healed the crippled,
Set bound men free.

Gods' perfect son,
The great I AM!
Shed holy blood,
To cover our sin.

Hope, peace and joy,
He offers all men.
Hear the bells ring,

Hallelujah Hallelujah!
Amen!

Three Words

And it is he who will supply all your needs from his riches in glory because of
what Christ Jesus has done for us. ~Phillipians 4:19 (TLB)

There are three words
I often say
To rise above
troubles
Of the day

These three words
They never fail
I'm lifted up
Peace prevails

As Peter walked
On stormy seas
When faith faltered
Jesus heard his pleas

"Help me Jesus"
Easy to say
When sadness comes
Fear blocks my way

So thankful may I always be
These three words
Safe harbor for me!

There Will Be Flowers

---◆◆◆---

He will wipe away all tears from their eyes, and there shall be no more death, nor sorrow, nor crying, nor pain. All of that has gone forever. ~Revelation 21:4 (TLB)

I think of all that awaits in heaven. Pearly gates, bright light, great riches and angelic hosts. But, far greater than any of these; the love of God will flow freely encompassing all who enter. No fear, no hate, heavenly peace!

Most of all and above all of this I will see Jesus! To gaze upon His face. I want to see Him but feel afraid to look.

Humbly, and wholly saturated with His presence!

I will be surrounded by the desires of my heart, loved ones, music, heavenly peace. I will dwell in a place of prophets and disciples…. astounding! God will know me! Imagine that! He has known me always before the world was made. His mark is upon me, and I am forever home in His heaven.

Heaven will be…words fail me! I'm sure there will be flowers!

The Sea of Life

I tremble at the enormous waves of the future rolling towards me. I'm sure I will perish!!! The surfer beside me is filled with expectation. He is trembling with anticipation. He can't wait to ride the wave!!! Lord may I be more like the surfer. I trust you to help me balance!

Waves

Today I hear
Waves of the sea
They speak of
your love for me

Ever present
when I do not hear
Crashing loud
to chide and steer

Grateful, thankful,
deep within
Your waves of love
Wash away my sin

So steady
they forever roll
Drawing in
my restless soul

Calm me now
my great God
But for a moment
here we trod

Upon this earth
With all its pain
You died, shed blood
Rose again

Making pure
refining us
A robe of white
Sweet righteousness

Thank you, thank you,
thank you, Jesus,
In your sacrifice
you saved us

Wave on wave
His mercy rolls
Restores again
my wayward soul

May I ever
seek your face
Cover me with
Your grace

I will forever
thankful be
Your waves of love
have covered me!

My Prayer

This is the day the Lord has made. We will rejoice and be glad in it.
~Psalm 118:24 (TLB)

I still myself.
I acknowledge your divine presence.

Quiet my lips.
Open my ears.
Inspire my thoughts.

In times of darkness,
You give light.

In times of anguish,
Hope!
I am forever humbled!

When confusion frustrates,
And panic ensues-
You open doors.

I seek to honour you in every word.

I praise and thank you
For guidance, never changing promises.
Your holy essence shared with me,
Forgiveness bestowed.

You are love.
You are joy.
You are peace.
I am forever grateful.
AMEN

Waiting

As for me, I look to the Lord for his help; I wait for God to save me; he will hear me. Do not rejoice against me, O my enemy, for though I fall, I will rise again! When I sit in darkness, the Lord himself will be my Light.
~Micah 7:7-8 (TLB)

This thing is hard!
This waiting on the Lord!
I want action and I want is now
NOW!
But I must wait with expectation;

I wait

I know my God hears me
He is my salvation
He has all the answers
He is the answer!

Though I am surrounded by darkness
there is light
The Lord never leaves me

Though I fall again and again and again
Jesus never leaves
He holds my hands and bids me to rise and stand
again and again!

I will wait

Yes this waiting thing is hard
It is a powerful teacher

It causes me to still my tongue
focus my attention in silence.

A soft breath on my soul
A Holy whisper in my ear.
Yes I am waiting
I will be silent in his Holy presence.

Many souls walk this earth
He knows each one
He desires each one to come to him
To grow in his mercy

To rise up and follow
He is light!
He is victory!
He reigns in power and majesty!

He hears the simple prayer
Of the broken and contrite
He bends low and listens

Yes I will wait

Though I seek answers now!

Perhaps not in my time,
But answers will come
His timing I can not question
I will be vigilant

And wait.

About the Author

Charlotte lives in Spruce Grove, Alberta, Canada.

Grandmother, mother, aunt and sister; her life is busy and interesting. She is an avid gardener, accomplished pianist, novice writer and terrible artist!

She has traveled extensively, volunteered at home as well as abroad. Charlotte has been a widow for many years yet says she has never been alone. Jesus is always with her calming her fears and shining a light on the path ahead.

She loves the quote Max Lucando wrote stating *the presence of anxiety is unavoidable, the prison of anxiety is a choice. Her prayers would be that you find encouragement in these words; that you would be drawn to scripture and choose to seek forgiveness and hope in Christ.*

Printed in the United States
by Baker & Taylor Publisher Services